BURN DIARY

POEMS

JOSHUA CHRIS BOUCHARD

Also by Joshua Chris Bouchard

ABRACADABRA (with Fawn Parker)
BORDERLINE DEFINITIONS
LET THIS BE THE END OF ME
PORTRAITS
WOOL WATER

BURN
DIARY

POEMS

JOSHUA CHRIS BOUCHARD

A Buckrider Book

Published by Buckrider Books
an imprint of Wolsak and Wynn Publishers
280 James Street North
Hamilton, ON L8R2L3
www.wolsakandwynn.ca

Editor for Buckrider Books: Paul Vermeersch
Editor: Liz Howard | Copy editor: Ashley Hisson
Cover and interior design: Kilby Smith-McGregor
Author photograph: Yuli Scheidt
Typeset in FreightText Pro and Dunbar Tall
Printed by Coach House Printing Company, Toronto, Canada

10 9 8 7 6 5 4 3 2 1

The publisher gratefully acknowledges the support of the Canada Council for the Arts and the Ontario Arts Council. We also acknowledge the financial support of the Government of Canada through the Canada Book Fund and the Government of Ontario through the Ontario Book Publishing Tax Credit and Ontario Creates.

Library and Archives Canada Cataloguing in Publication

Title: Burn diary : poems / Joshua Chris Bouchard.
Names: Bouchard, Joshua Chris, author.
Identifiers: Canadiana 20230496423 | ISBN 9781989496732 (softcover)
Subjects: LCGFT: Poetry.
Classification: LCC PS8603.O92414 B87 2023 | DDC C811/.6—dc23

I am warming my cold
hands at the dancer's
ruby eye –
the fire, the suddenly discovered knowledge of love.

– SHARON OLDS, "Satan Says"

BURN

DIARY

Miracle

I am born in the holy milk of my mother's eyes,
and she calls me *Electric, Moment, Dumbbell,*
Fever. Severed from black muscle of hollow
bone, the earth pries my fists and they hold
me in their image. *This is a sacred rite and now*
you belong to the earth. Thank you, I now succumb
to the world. I learn to clean my hair with vinegar
and spit, slowly in time, then expertly
in my father's house. He builds conical nests,
reads his paperback, caresses my body with his mouth.
Lethargy, he says, *is a terrible sin.* She asks
him where the others went, as he clears a hole in the
branches, opens a glass bin of ghosts: teeth, skulls,
carapaces, eyebrows, tufts of hair. They were called
prisoners, threaded behind the rib cage
under her blouse and undone sutures – still, impure.
Bootlegging lives like criminals, they teach me
where they keep fault lines at the ends of dull
days, as they bathe me in the golden hem of the sun,
feed me berries and eggplants, call my names.

Dissemination

The ocean has purpose.
Saying *the past is the past* is useless.

I don't have much, but a body has its benefits.
Smooth roll of the surf.
Empty space in a trough.

The ocean opens and shuts like a window.
The thing is, I've only ever seen it.

Once I put my toes in a wave.
Chaos as it inhaled.
But that's it.

One way or the other, things overflow.
What *things*?

If you want something, fight for it.
I was told to hear myself before I speak.
You can't just take a voice once it's there.

Whatever the ocean takes, it gives back.
Right?

Irony has its uses, but lays flat like a jellyfish.
Reminds people to pay attention.

Describing the ocean is useless.
Most people already know how to disappear.

Procession

Natural causes. I read back the revisions
of your literature, receding hairline, French

accent: fledged by your little daughters.
Hot breath cringing in the lake behind

the house, steak for breakfast, wood lawns
to spread on. A part of me came from

your cock, a part of me came from
your hands, a part of me came from

the old back roads. Where the girls
crawled out to kiss their lonely fathers.

Animals

What I feel is what I always mean.
Against broken moving parts.

Writhe is all I should do.
Be those animals moaning in sun fur.

We mean to slam our arches on backbones.
Strike piles of flint with our teeth.

We can be a dog flapping its unhinged jaw.
Sometimes we are even all its spit.

Sometimes at night we burn like houses.
Bored in the rabid yellow foam of fuck.

We are brave but hide within each other.
We become everything that is holy shit.

How to Tear a Partridge Apart

Ask Daddy to show you how to hunt it. It's always wet
in the moss, he tells you, and the tracks of the half-born
calves lead you to open nests. They're all idiots struck
by thunder. It should be October. It should be morning.
It should be calm and feel like aching. Inside the trails,
ask him how to finger coagulated sap from pine trees,
put it in your mouth and chew it like gum. *Just like this*,
he says. Nature's blood candy. Walk for hours. Enough
to collapse under the weight of your backpack. Hold
the rifle in your arms like a newborn and coo. Stop
at a muskeg, but he doesn't call it a muskeg, and scan
the covey. See them bobbing their heads, lazy and dumb,
and point at them. Treat them like your children. Watch them
swoon in ditches. Pick one, any one, because they're all
the same, lifelike but not quite real. Replace your hand
with the rifle and aim. Point at their eyes. Always remember
that the good meat is the breast meat – it must be shot clean
and free of pellets or lead. See the breaking sun. See
the crosshairs. See the finger rest on the crescent-moon
trigger. When the aim is right, shoot. If it strikes, you'll see
blood on the grass. Watch their brothers and sisters
hide in the echo. Put your hands on its body. Stuff it
in a plastic bag. Shake Daddy's hand when he says, *Good*.
Bring the carcass back to camp, the one that shadows
the dead lake, and put the carcass on leaves by the logs,
the empty shore. Hold the partridge upside down by its feet.
Rest the head just above the ground, spread its limp wings with
your heels. Place your boots over each and grip the skin,
and when he says, *Do it*, rip out the legs from the body.
The slow threat of flesh, ripped from feathers, as the inside
separates from breastbone, the hidden parts once intact

at the pelvis, and the only things left are the head and feet.
The dull knife still cuts through hollow bone. Throw
the gizzards into a shallow hole, but he doesn't call it a hole,
and wash the breast meat in a basin. The guts signal foxes.
The blood attracts turtles. But you don't kill those things.
Daddy cuts the meat into strips, prepares the pan with
butter and oil. Keep the feet as souvenirs. Pull at tendons,
make the talons open and shut, pretend the secret thing
it came from once had life. You laugh deep in the woodshed,
sharpen knives with spit. One day soon, you'll hate all of this.

Violence

Take birds home and attach
them on cliffs with wire. Concrete
heads like the temple size
of your heart, shards of beak, remnants
of stunted growth. Your memory
is sharp now, teeth cut in shoals
in your mouth. Wet sinews of

that mouth, reflections of meat
trespassing from interiors
moulded into shape with talons,
painted onto dirt. Discarded
feathers, eyes, soft guilt.
Forget where you buried
the remains.

Jazz

You tell me how to hurt myself with spoons.
You keep bathwater in jars on the porch.
I used to be your unhinged silly dumbo.
Sometimes you find me hiding in a hole.
I used to pretend I couldn't move.
You showed me home movies about avalanches.
Your fingers held thread against my hands.
The radiator is on full blast.
You fall asleep on my tiny white thighs.
I'm grateful when you check if I pissed myself.
We're old now and live far from our memories.
You tell me you miss the glint in my eyes.
You know all my sins.

Bloodlines

I dream of basketball nets tangling the horned earwigs.
My grandmother and her baked-rhubarb effigy.

When I'm spinning out of control, I call it leaning
right in. My sister raising her eyebrows in the living
room, her heavy body like stained wool.

It's all natural, like birth or water
or deer at dusk in the rut, moths awestruck
by lamplight. Her fingers gripping at my neck.

The moment I felt my hands in the fire of my life
was when I put them in you and taught myself to be
a hell king.

She shows my blood in her hands and baby garter snakes
she pulls from traps. She begs to be forgiven.

I forget where I hid the notebooks. Without them
I'd never know her anatomy, little strips left of me to eat.

It could have been much worse without the words.
We forgive those who made it feel so perfect.

Abandonment Season

I haven't been well
lately. I'm not always
eating my greens, folding
my clothes, extracting those
cysts. My mother is sick.
A wolf dressed in knives. Soon
it will be spring.

I Hate that Journey for You

Fishing on Pear Lake at dawn
I had a knife for nothing.

A bear or wolf in broad light,
too scared to walk to the generator.

In the shadow of the shed it was placed
under the cedar, evergreen and water lines

before the clearing where they came.
Two men over the hill on a four-wheeler.

On the lake I raised my hand to wave
and they returned, my knife felt smooth

between my legs where it was neatly placed.
I gutted the fish as the men drove away.

Travelling safe back to the dark –
the men were effortless.

Burial

A path is always drawn. I see it
beyond fallen snow. A row of blades

above a broken knee of land. Winter
sheds around me: finger snap, moan,

binge-drinking moon. From a distance,
the hours arriving home approach longing

and I'm laughing at the loss.
Chewed sinew of hinterland, crushed

ash of bone. The bruised shore
keeps lakes from thawing. This path

is open: memory, asleep
in a snow tunnel. Huddled to the wall,

shaded from cold, I was removed.
That could be now

but for regret, the split of tinder
and hearing snow buckle in. It takes

a step to make a footprint, trails already laid.
Roads flash into blindness, but to where?

Heritage Site

You can be something all you want.
I earn the burn. Among the open-flower

chests of my mothers and my fathers
and my brothers and my sisters. Their

terrible heads smashed together, the sun
wilting flakes of itself like prepared fish.

The highlands of the town flow into lakes,
rocks blown by dynamite, a heritage site

for the discovery of fire. Miracles every day:
a man gives birth to a 4 x 4 truck, a dog learns

to use a jackleg, a woman implodes inside
the gut of a goose.

Erosion of the grassroot beats their dreams
in sleep, far inside the dark earth, helmet

flashlights illuminate a glimpse of a secret
inner sea. They say it's just a legend, even when

they see it with their own eyes. I beg them for
this kind of denial reserved only for the heroic,

heirlooms stamped onto their faces. They lose
children in hidden backyard wells, flash

their genitals to the graveyards of their fathers.
This town is dying but the sun keeps rising.

Deep underground, light disappears into rock.
Hands born to bleed, but young bodies heal quickly.

Help

At Dairy Queen, you lifted your shirt over your head,
showed me the cancer scars on your chest.

I made a large cone but fucked up the swirly tip
and gave it to you for free. It was raining.

The last time I saw you we smoked pot
from a cracked Coke can behind a church.

You showed me your life like almost nothing
I've shown you. How did you survive it all?

Behind the hockey arena? In buckets of sand filled
with cigarettes? When I punched you in the face, pornos

at the bleachers, dirty weed we stole from your dad?
I could see it as you walked away, the sun broke

in the clouds just above you as you disappeared
over the hill, like bad movies we talked about at the lake.

I'm sorry I left and became the hipster sellout asshole
we said we'd never be. With no real scars to show you.

I Am Well

I always cared lovingly
shooting the .22-gauge, shooting
true with the good ammo
that exploded into shrapnel
upon impact, and I always carefully
tied the paddleboat
with a knot I saw my grandmother
tie, bothered to learn the bends
of dirt logging roads,
checked the doors were locked
before leaving, the propane
and water tanks were closed, shades
drawn tight to keep furniture
from bleaching. I always looked back
from the truck's rear window
for one last look, when the foxes
came out to eat the partridge parts,
and it was always the same
when I returned, because I never
saw my reflection in the lake.

Now I'm breathing heavily
at Frank and Oak, buying expensive
IPA, and I move in the streets
like a doppelgänger,
with my pants rolled up,
my beard short or long, and I linger
in theatres and cafés as they brim
and reach like conifers, pines, birches.
Everyone I know asks me, How are you,
and I tell them, I am well,
as we meet at heritage houses, parks'
splintered benches.

A man
behind the coffee counter tells me:
You can drown
in just two inches of water, a puddle
or a bathtub or a river,
that it's only a matter of
being awake, before I stretch
my hand toward the streetcars
moving like snakes, hissing
like snakes, turning us
in their bodies, and the bends
look the same from the seats,
embedded tracks, every definite
departure.

Suffering Migration

When one life ends, another begins.
Born in wildfires, floods and burning
seas, the half-rot marrow of bone.

Whereas I, supplemented in the kink
of a spine, regress tangentially into
the fold of its caress: the motherfucker.

After all, I think getting therapy was the
best idea, all things considered. Her
with a box of tissues on the side table,

the analog clock grinding behind me
signalling only the end: for her, a marker
of one death to the next, blunt refusal.

This weekend the hostess of the party
mentioned to me again in passing: life is
what you make of it, an endless ocean.

Good to know, I said, many thanks for the
invitation, where everyone I know
shits out the bullet, climbs the ladder.

Don't lie to me, both of us deserve better.
Wave to the dead on your way through
tomorrow: this city, faces, brutal necessity.

I Am Also the Night

I am the house's abandoned
rooms and I am the open window.

In long hours I stay broken
with the night lights

and give them my open hands.
I say, *Please make me whole*

but only if I am worthy.
Sometimes I dream of electric tombs,

puzzled bodies and my photograph
of the night. I bend my body back

and open my eyes wide,
say, *Ah, I am also the photograph.*

The lies of me I learn to keep
like heirlooms in cold corners

and imagine how it feels to be
only a name, a single body.

I hate the night, but I am also
the night, and I am barely human

in the tender carnage of daybreak.
I never see it coming

as it unfurls from the ends of my teeth
and paints the walls with light

and I kneel. *Thank you for not killing me,*
there's still so much to live in.

Birds Fly into the Mouth of the Sun

Birds fly into the mouth of the sun.
When birds learn to fly, all they do is jump
and their bodies do the rest. Some of them
die from the fall, but some live.
The living ones nestle in bricked holes,
unrecognizable, chew pebbles and rock-hard bread,
break the hollow bones of their siblings.
The lucky ones burrow their heads
under wings, sift straw-twig homes, sing
when the sun rises and sets, the moon rises and sets.
It's easy to feel brave when we see them above us
flying somewhere south. We ask how far they'll go,
how far to come back, will they even make it?
In a V, birds follow the birds in front of them, and
the bird in the centre follows their own blind will.
They know each other by the sounds
they make when alone.

Little Lake

We burn our names in traplines.
Forests smaller than faces.

I mark the trail with a scarf.
Trees collapse at the bowl of milk.
We have language, but not measurement.

.

Pierre is talking in his sleep, acting out his fuck dreams.
He writhes in sun-laced mud, fully clothed, dumb.
He rubs his face and head, and chokes.

.

My body washes onto a shore of deer antlers.

.

Jamie jerks to the periphery of clear-cut stumps.
He counts the dead ages, hula-hoops the rings.
My hands are carved from axe blades.

.

It was really nice hating you. – Agatha

I put the bark on a dried block and skin it.
She rips the sheets from bent monarchs.
I tie a dandelion stem into a knot.

Saplings push out the heads of new birth.

.

Jamie and I list everything we want for:

Slivers	Drum sets
Koans	Horsetails
Cedar	Crayons
Kissing	Timelessness
Hot baths	Cookie batter
Damp moss	Loon calls

I forgot "Sleep," he says.
I have loved and kept my eyes soft.

.

Pierre thinks on a moon-bent cock, inside out.
He sees himself in dreams, scrapes chunks of cloud.

We ask him, *Do you dream of the setting sun?*
Do you dream of hands that lay you?

His mouth opens, teeth carved into dream catchers.

.

We bet Jamie a moose tongue:
You cannot finish a painting in under an hour.

He finishes almost instantly.
He holds it up above his head like a square halo.
A portrait of a mirror reflecting wet chalk lines.

.

Agatha offers me a box wrapped in birch.
This is for gurgling the snowmelt.

I unfurl the birch, collect the scraps.
I open the box and see a dawn-calm lake.
A beaver cleans its ass, a loon washes her dead.

.

Jamie lies sleepless in the trunk of a split cedar.
Pierre wraps himself in the cold of crabgrass.
Agatha draws a door in the overgrown milkweed.

.

I float toward the trail with a handful of twigs.
Hold the scarf and look upon the threshold.

.

Here is everything I owe you.

Lumina

How loons talk: call
in lily pads
trapped in murk.

Fires lit, fingernail flints
before trees put to sleep
in long-told stories

culled in flame.
Call,   listen
for pitches of love

in another
walking pitfall, lummoxes of land.
Sing,

endure bodies if learned to do
what moons do – disappear
in phases like fireflies,   Morse code

light returned.
Loons live thirty years or more
in sleep, dream

of lives lost if not for mirth,
sound, each other's lover
lodged inside the night.

Sleep Mask

Tell them the dreams of crystal cliffs,
licking ridges off wooden sheets

hanging from my clothesline before
the cleared scape of dumb mountains.

As I fall into the man's house
among body sculptures playing dead,

pretending to pass away on glass beds
carved in hills by diamond hands.

The mountains bloom
inside my eyelids.

All the Places Look Like Forest Fires

The places you take me smell
like animals. You show me blood
near the clearing and uncover rib cages.
Once, you held up the head of a black bear
and imitated its death with its jaw,
carefully described the buckshot or disease
or poison inside inedible red berries.
You told me about the history of love.
The first time I fell in love I saw children
picking up trash from the edges
of the highway, and I saw you posing
next to deer antlers, birds, taxidermied
sculptures of horses and pigs and dogs.
Sometimes when the grass is long enough
you let insects spread on your neck and
you tell me that they won't hurt you
because you made them with your body.
The first time I fell in love
I meant to tell you that I couldn't stand it.
The places look like forest fires, cauterized
into memories of our tired fathers
when we were born, fields near our houses
that burned. The point to all of this, you
tell me, is to make it all into something
less shameful, press it into our mouths
until the young are well enough to leave us.
The last place you take me is under the bed,
where you hide all the others, figurines
who talk like the heads of dead animals
rotting at the base of the tree line, waiting
for you to collect them.

Letters to Lost Children

My good friend is dead.
She took pills and she was old
and had a bad heart. It was pills,
I think, but nobody tells me anything.
We need to get together soon. This summer
we should meet back home and I could cook,
use my recipes, like at the barbecues
when you were young and there
were water-balloon fights. It was the year
it was so hot both of your ears
got sunburned and blistered and we used
that aloe vera gel. It was hard
but you seemed happy. Even when you
got poison ivy after walking
without a shirt in the bushes.
We put oven mitts on your hands
to stop you from scratching.

Honey, if you want, I promise
not to talk. We could just eat.
I got a new job, but lost it.
I got the internet and went on the Job Bank
and got a job. I hope you're proud.
It was at Value Village and I hurt my back.
I couldn't stand the smell of old clothes
and leather. Those are all dead
people's clothes, did you know?

Honey, I miss my friend.
I love you and think about you.
Say hello to your girl for me. Say hello
to her and pretend we still have something
to show for our blood, the good years
on Frame Crescent and the park
with the giant boulder right in the middle.

They tore that old park down, I heard,
but the boulder is still there. Why move it.
Why spend the time. I haven't heard
from you, but I'll wait, and I know
your sister will let me know how you are.

I sent you a message on Instagram.
You're getting old. I'm getting so old.
Like everyone, I guess, the whole world.
When we meet, tell me stories, tell me things.
Oh, have you heard? My dad died.
My dad is dead and my friend is dead.
The whole world is dying.
Time moves so quickly, it's dizzying.
All this life.

I Think of Thought

When I think of thought
    I think of
street lines that show me to you.
Time stopping at the hearse
of light, roots beneath concrete
over earth's soft structures.
Stars lend themselves
only to you, a borrowed gift
to return.
    I always think of
how you saw me with a life
intact, sutured by its own
weight of flowers. How you
followed me back.
    You think of the world
and create it in your image:
nearly perfect, alive, love dreamt
in the hide of daybreaks.
    You live inside
the burrows and mend them with
your movements, edge to edge,
in action. You ask nothing of love,
like music in the empty arenas
of our chests.
    I think of you
thinking of me, how we'll
never die.

Stet

When I say *thank you*, I mean
I can't go on like this.

A body has many variations.

Once I followed the street lines
to the little shores of suck.

The parody of being wide open
is the invitation.

Your mouth has a tasteless look.

I have made many mistakes, I have
dog-eared the inconceivable folds.

When you walk all over me, I think
See you again tomorrow, again.

Bring me to your keeper.

There is a new figure when I sleep,
but the moment has passed.

Palms lay spread like open fields.
If it's not broken, break it until it is.

This is all very dangerous.

Burn Diary

Clear the path of willow trees,
aboard the train to the city of ghosts.

Curl into my soft-blue resected knot
and burn there, like a road flare

on an abandoned highway.
I make my choices; I hold them high.

Like statues or graves, chalk outlines
of what's even worse than absence.

Valedictory

I tape a cardboard photograph
of a deer in a meadow on the window
and begin. The deer's leg is broken

at the knee, it is snorting at the grass,
it is giving birth to the dead. Machines
work by mimicking

real movements. When the deer dies
it is replaced by a bear, a snake,
then insects eating the sweet yellow

sugar of piss. Wherever I am I must
understand that animals only work
by following me to the end of life. I mourn

their passing as I put my fingers inside
their gears to make them go, and if they
do not go, I sound out the phases

of their lives. It is a miracle I can work
this long without them biting at apples
in the muskegs. The sun burns

a hole through the photograph, fades
the paper as it turns translucent – a ghost deer –
until all that is left is the window, and you

on the lawn kissing grass. I eat the cardboard
with a knife and fork, bury my best draft.
You don't believe this, and I don't believe me.

Summer

My red-hot ass burns to lick
melting ice cream from your fingers
at dusk in the park on a swing set,

bucking myself wild and barrelling
near the cathedrals of blood puddles,
just along the parkettes of where
I have met you.

The lampshades are heavy again.
My body in the pool of liquid sugar,
candy thrown from black-canvas tote bags.

Mouths of awestruck newlyweds spread
in sunscreen catching seeds under dumb-fuck
half-moons, groping themselves like choirs in heat,
taking a giant piss on the canopy of eyelashes.

We lose everything:
the will to smoke and shop and eat and read,
pretending to live forever on feathers
wet with firecracker white-light plumage.

Woe is me walking toward the picnic table
eating a rotten fig like an apple-stuck piglet,
and that's all very good because it is summer,
motherfucker, it is always bright and spit-shined.

As I point to the sky,
my right temple,
this place.

When I Walk into an
Air-Conditioned Dollarama

I feel like punching myself in the face
to make sure I have a destiny, and I walk
straight to the toiletries aisle because
I am unclean, unfit to touch or feel the
air on my palms, ramming red party cups
with my fingers full of stink, smearing
white porcelain bowls with the runoff
salty discharge, because I am so unclean,
look at how unclean I am, licking buckets,
holding mops upside down and dancing
with my face in the thick braided bristles,
look at how happy I am doing a tarantella
before I shove duct tape rolls and zip-ties
into my mouth and I choke and vomit on
the floor, run up and down, paint my face
in dirty milk chocolate melted on my knees,
grab everyone by the shoulders and scream,
Oh look at this thing as I pass away I love it.

Controlled Burn

Barely standing there
on four legs, body
stuck in a mound of flame.

Somebody left you
upside down and rotting,
chipped and torn

by weather. We put
you out of your gull, push
you over the roots of

red and green pines,
stoke the pit with brush.
It isn't hard to throw

you in, dissolve this
all into the soil, black
plastic under paint.

You are calm when
engulfed in smoke, cut
from your severed hinges.

Like a Buddha or a saint,
ash slowly replaces the air,
hands collect it like basins.

I Get Stoned Again

At Angel Lake near the big hill
under the sun, where the bear skull rots,

I get stoned again. I stand on concrete slabs
of an abandoned dock and feel calm.

I don't want to live without loving you.

I can't resolve to keep a good life. I rot
with the bear skull in the straw, concrete,

heaps of trash at the base of the shore.
I let nature have me in its maw. I hope

I am worthy of this sacred passage.

11:11

Inside the warm gooey centres of
our old house, frames built by bent kneecaps

at the eroded pulpits of trusses. Negative space
of voice meets wood, concrete, linoleum,

glitter from birthday bath bombs. We all
must honour the rooms – revolutions of

bodies cleaned by perforated tongues
of flame. Everything here works as

it should. The clock outlines the numbers
in radiant neon green beneath our eyes.

Light from the oven, bedside table, handheld
visions of night. Patterns in a soupy fugue,

miracles in the toilet bowl, insects silently
jotting your movements from one room

to the next: oceans. Make a wish to the sun.
Sun: grant us the wish of this disbelief.

The Hand that Feeds Me

Will kill me if I suck on it. Tonight
the fingers drip in the ashy afterglow
of a secret life, yellow tape around
the palm of a dead scene. I used to see it
coming for me, track black-bloom ruins,
trace bruises on my skin. It used to feed
me whatever I showed it: swings, soap,
black-cherry gumballs, the miracle of my birth.
As sickness shakes the weather of its passing,
the hand feels for wounds. Digging
the narrow spine of earth – honey, flowers –
gifts for the empty creases of my skin.
The tectonic shift of my hips as I walk
the runway toward the perfect boundary,
dressed in my best to impress the fisted bulge:
Am I doing this right? The hand knows
where I sleep at night, but I've never been good
at betrayal. But it's simple when I know
where the hand has been. Buried in the wet drag
of a crawl, dirt leaves finer imprints than spit.
So good now at following the come-hither
of the finger but I never thought I'd get this far.
I must have seen it coming but did nothing,
an endless history. Desperation is a violent breed.

Shrike

How you navigate
open places. The grip

of your hands is the holy mirror
where the mind stretches.

Sometimes I think
I always meet you at the wrong moments.

I've tried to feel the hours like
threads, fight for good people

and love between bookends
of bodies. Pain, however necessary, can't last.

When I'm slipping into the long mornings
it's almost always to find you,

because when I swallow my tongue
and choke, I know its worth –

you might be listening. You'll be laughing
in stray light. You'll leave this place

and I think, Hear my call
in the endless years of living.

Sharpshooter

Slumming it in the deepest
burrows, shoulders dressed in
boulders. Below the hill near
your father's grave, this is
what you remember: sunken in
death, burned in the mouth by it,
bar soap covered in hair. Violence
is a good story, don't you know?
Sometimes a path to knowing,
sometimes, a life. Burdened
targets keep moving. Swing sets
unravel their chains.

Beg

Feel the grooves of your teeth when the lights are off.

Split enamel bathroom sinks stick beneath my chin.

We live hyena in our apartment built with neon ash.

You slinky inside the rooms and stamp your hands.

We fold half of what we own.

When you crouch near the windows I just pummel.

Push the crown moulding with my heels.

Take my hair in your palms and pull.

Tomorrow we are heading to YUL.

Tonight we stare down pockmarks in the popcorn ceiling.

You find a yellow centipede and balance it on your knuckles.

Is this everything, you ask.

Please just tell me.

Nil by Mouth

I hate when people call it *a voice*,
a noise to make us clean.

I try to pick a hair off its tongue.
It swallows. Overhead lights make it

look already dead. It shouldn't be here
stuffed in gauze and coughing but

I saw it in a vision standing at its feet,
palms frozen in ice chips.

I wouldn't let them touch it
still. Knotted hair, ingrown nails, half-lit eyes.

Starving for anything real, solid,
without consequence. Anything that can wither

and pass through it. Sometimes I forget
it's morning and sleep forever beside it,

dreaming of windows. It's always different
but it's like it has me beneath its arms.

I don't think this room can hold it. Nothing
will take back how we pushed our faces

in its lap, hid deep in its secret quiet.
It's morning and this time it has left us.

You Are Getting Married

When I practise at playing God,
I place my steps in your footprints.
I am preparing for winter. I am waiting

for when you tell me that you are
getting married, and I am preparing
for you to describe your husband's mouth.

I will slip into the longing ephemera
when you text me the name of your new father.
I have spun you from black thread. I want

to beat your husband and I want him to
describe every mark I've made on his neck.
If you cannot find him, he is here. He is

beneath me, under pulpits and light
and the land rolling into firm softness.
Once I had a dream of your torso in the air,

you had the look of a confident person,
your husband was spinning. In time
he will suddenly die with me.

The Lie

In endless
descriptive detail,
like bad novels,
I can't
stress enough
how much
I love you.
Stress to crush
the legs of horses,
this body
on the white duvets
of our nail beds.
The disaster of
our hearts,
I thought I'd get
away with it.
So clever, hidden,
I bet my dick on it.

Leaf Blower

As a child, I thought they all just appeared
and disappeared. Like adults in the house
who, for fun, dressed as ghosts on weekends
with sheets from the linen closet, deceived
almost no one, not even the young ones.
They bloomed at the turn of every season
and fell, gave birth to abandoned silhouettes.
Now I study the batch of spider eggs attached
behind the woodshed in the backyard,
decide whether they are worth living, knowing
the silky sacs of breathing bulbs will tear apart
in the manufactured wind. They, too, just appeared.
But it's not my fault. It never is. They have a job
to do and so do I. The spider and the leaves
and the weeds all have their own versions
of living, which is to avoid death, or at least,
fall into it. I turn on the engine, point the nozzle
at their web and piles of decay, see my neighbours
from their windows, curtains half-drawn, silently
judge me. I apologize. It's 7:00 a.m. and I have to live.
I have to kill everything around me or else
be killed, mourn the fake ghosts who taught me
not to be frightened of anything, not even
of them, not of you. I will teach my children.

The Master

I meant to show you –
but I forgot.
Was it to be a man
unknown to himself? I meant
to make our home
acceptable only to you,
perfect for the task.
Carpets need sweeping,
dishes need washing –
somebody needs do it.
Somebody's got to arrange
the whole damn house
for thirty years straight.
Polish the slanted blade
of the guillotine.
I propose to be
useful only in your eyes.
Flawless, at least, in
the darkness.

Milk Teeth

Diorama
milk machine, blood
factory. Glands
on rust. Honey
jaws of life, blow
into melted glass.
Make the
monument. Teeth
are earned
in sport,
compare crotches.
Fuck the knot.
Hope
you've given up.
Story of my life: this
under the bedside
window.
Bodies keep growing
and I am death, I am
cauterized. Give
me release,
tanned fur. Make me
earn my keep.

The Hours Are Beautiful Nests

I don't want what you want,
but give me the hours.

There are decoy songs in the bush.
They mimic dreams and rolling wood.

Our names bump in the trees.
The nests are separate futures, islands.

We see the distance suddenly close.
Measure ourselves by invented increments.

Wind, sand and swollen metal scraps.
We've somehow collected the obvious.

My body stands as an open witness.
We need to tear this place apart.

Monuments

It felt clean to write of the backdropped
clouds, steak and eggs, dirt roads outside
Rocky's café where I saw a ship
take sail by the Trans-Can. Drove to
the 108 south in a school bus. Lakes
of snow absent of footprints, a quiet
could clean itself of history. Even
the road swallowed. It was a lie when
I said that I was never coming back.
Up to the city buried in rock mined
by the men of my father's day, ash
of ghost birds like tendrils strangling
the highway – they erected monuments to
the dead. When I arrived, I checked for
my father's name, but it wasn't there. I saw
plaques beneath the drift lines and saw
my own name, statues at the edge of
the hills boarded by Horne Lake.
I grabbed for rope in my pocket and heard
a boom, saw the sky unravel.
I undulated and sifted near the shore.
When the time was right, I moved deep
in trees, pulled the rope, tied it to my wrists.
I showed my palms, checked the lines.
Okay, I said, *I'm ready now.*
Take me there.

I Want to Ask the Therapist

When am I going to die?

I'm doing all the work.
I'm moving from room to room.

I want to ask the therapist,
Tell me what you really believe?

Watch the body quickly suffer.
In my black-denim petals of smoke.

Breath of their unending advice.
Inside the boring, reflective white room.

I want to be subjected to their will.
A dog as it humps a stuffed animal.

All humble beginnings: stainless skin
like sheet metal in a sea of pollen.

I want to ask the therapist,
Can you please forgive me?

I am so useless, innocent and brave.
I do all the work and ask for your love.

Spread the seed of my ancient thought.

Gangue Extraction

Regret of unearned loss. Sick

of thought at the lake of tailings, bird

sanctuaries at creeks. Grown

from deposited light, assaulted roads.

You beneath cloud-covered dark in

a Pontiac Sunfire, stained in moss, lay

a map of ore on the seat. Fate is your

departure home. Sweaty palms,

honest talk. We kiss like broken glass.

Interrogated by regret, we abandon

our bodies, extract rock

from memory. Flinching at red murk,

this demonstration, a wave of recognition.

Only this shadow we bear to outline.

What I May Have Been if I Had Been There

With you in the front cab, the windows up,
cigarette smoke filling the red canvas seats,
radio turned up loud to any song by AC/DC,
which I might have known you liked if I had
known you. If I had been there with your seat
belt undone, empty cans of Molson Canadian
and some thought about what you would see
if you had made it through. If I had been there,
wings of crickets and fireflies headed straight
for us, the mines both hid behind and beyond,
only one more day's drive home. What I may
have been if I slept in the thick arms of asphalt.
Apart from you in work but with you in time.
We could have at least bled together, bent cut
metal with our faces in awestruck guises, our
arms frozen by headlights, and I could have woke
you before the smoke or the horn of a semi with
no one in the cab but a driver, alone like you. If
I had been there to fall with you as it struck the
tin-can chassis as the wheels jackknifed and
our heads broke just above our necks, and the
crushed grass stamped in hot engines, our legs
snapped behind our backs and the blue-red
gyroscope sirens like party lights. If I had talked
you out of sleep I would not be here living my
life without you, partly saved to remember us.

Despite the Meaning of All Things

Maybe the table will break from the weight of candlelight.
There are holes in plastic cups from impatient hands.

You ask me how I am holding up and I say, *Good*
and you ask me again and I say, *Good*, and you ask again

and I say, *How about another shot, the moon is convulsing.*
I don't know what poetry is or what other people think it is.

The mark cannot be hit and I have cold hands and a bad eye.
It's good to look at the CN Tower and hovering green lights.

Someone turns and says, *What's the quiet one's name*
and someone answers for me and this is the end of knowing.

Everything that happens here is from impulse.
I sit in this chair with the deliberateness of a newborn.

The host is studying linguistics and I ask if there's a word for *This*.
He offers me pot in a beer can but it's too hard now to let go.

I see three people sitting silently in a dark room and I want
to know what it feels like to be satisfied with dying.

Tomorrow I am going to start again and file my teeth into matches.
Before I came here I read five poems that I didn't understand.

I promise to read them later before I stuff them under my tongue.
The black fire of the pages will justify my absence.

Blackfly

Let's be truthful: my mind
is only a centre. I have
smoothed out the unfinished
corners of my attachments.
When I fall, I deep-dive into
my empty coffee cup,
the soft morning of regret.
Let day consume
itself and collapse neatly into
my hands. For example,
now it is raining. Now,
I am inside.

Corporeal

Teach me a lesson now.

Figures in dark mornings. I see
shoddy murals carved in soft parts.
Fractured necks, sounds

I make when breathing.
I'm a big young baby boy.
I make sickness with metal hinds.

There are signs in skin, some
legible, mostly unread. I lay them
out in tiny paper strips. Maps
lead me to roads I've already built.

If you ask me how I do it, I say, *Severity.*
All I need is time beyond time. You call me:
Skin Fade, Mutt, The Thing I Put Back In.

I have the rest of my life to feel alive.

Hell King

The good hand takes you
to the deep down –

the forbidden highway.

Blood in your cereal bowl.
The peephole stuffed in gauze.

The carpenter measures twice.

Trust Fall

I will unravel.

Catharsis is my middle name.

I'm going supernova in the blind.

The gauge is the open lung, palm, skin I cut myself in.

I hear it coming in the tender heat of the body bag.

Never has it been as good as this.

I see a picture of *Cassini* hurtling into Saturn.

I want to extend my hand and stop it from death.

I sleep motionless in paper myths.

When I feel like hurtling, I trust fall into nowhere.

Until you extend your hand.

Mould me into the hollow of your spine.

I have said too much.

Hot Knives

She blacks out butter knives, smokes
stainless steel on vintage stovetops. She
crushes hot knives between her thighs,
tattoos herself in sulphur. Gets that
shit in before the door opens. Kisses
her kids. Puts the cat down. I think
she drags out the blades from her hip bones,
gives them names, never throws them away.
Collected in drawers ajar as markers for
burned-down houses on the hill where
she made her promises. The stink I know
is her heavy hand over the fire, singed hairs,
her body softening in air like a ruin.
Let the kids sit on your lap and slowly
suffocate with you.

Host

The insect bloats its shiny belly,
the insect's perfect mouth
cleans open orifices.

My mother has abandoned me
and I have abandoned her.

It dreamed of this life
in the schoolyard, a mirror
planted into its head.

It has grown large enough to curl
in the ears of warm human carriers,
make nests out of wool.

It lives well in this destruction.
I have abandoned the morning light.

Autodidact

The brave butcher the good horse.

Calm voices when they kill each other. Bodies curated
from stuck hooks, land masses beaten into submission.
In marbled, steak-cut flanks,

shadows of teeth stick in finer points: I put my mouth
in the shape of a barrel and curse the blessedness.
Between our black-tarred fingers

we break to caulk the severed fields. With you,
in keyholes and autodidacts, I ask the wrong questions.
Close of knives, the road to my heart

is black lined. Sometimes I hear you say, *It's a curse
to know you.* You paint faces on sheets and swoon, skim
cartilage bone. Dry me out on wood. Animals look at us

like playthings, and you let them. You don't let me take
the wet, cured fringe. Bashed-in heads on the grass edge.
The secret place you drag the lake or salt hill –

you lead me. You show me the way but never
what it takes to kill silently, sharpen on black stone.
When I learn it, you grade it. Pin red ribbons on my neck.

I am never wrong and mean it when you show me the good hand.

Thick Skin

A secret code of body language, furrowed brows.
Glances depending on who was near.
I am frightened because I never questioned
my own answers. Even when you never asked.
I slumped in the dark sheets behind drawn
drapes and knuckles. I am sending this to you
as a reminder for what needs none. As I remember
the bent grain of bedposts, hard pit of my soft organ,
paper-thin walls bounded by shadow.
You who wrapped me in dishevelled fur,
sticky from sweat and ambrosia, sighs of my dead laugh.
You who knew my sense of smell could not recognize
the stillborn between our legs, ghosted murk
more natural to me than how the sun sank.
You changed, impeccably crept in walls, like waking
from a fever. For once I wasn't afraid.
I slept in the dream-sake inside your chest
but could not dig the thick skin of your rib cage,
unfinished notes to yourself. We read the letters
when you took my virginity, crammed in empty orifices,
fished out with your tongue, stapled to the creases
of my knees. My mind is empty now, the code is broken.
I have broken it through distant rooms.

I Am Sick

My skin is tethered to long bolts.

Pinned by corners like teenage posters.

Say to me that my hands are bloodlines.

Make my death tiny smeared edges.

Today I am sick but I am also clean.

In the tidy rooms of our monuments.

Homes erected by miners and nurses.

Push me open in their secret hallways.

Up against their blowing-horror faces.

Show me the smallness of my open body.

Pigs

Pigs drink from the same lakes as dogs.

My mother was brave.
I wonder how many drugs she spent on beaches.
How she could throw her body on the sandhills.

I was fucked to life on Halloween night.
She put her hands in the shape of a cup, turned
to my father: *This is where your sun will live.*

This is where wet mouths of earth will bury him.
Over scratched fingers, his clothes will dissolve.
You are his father now until the day you die.

When you die, a little piece of me will die.
Space in these palms will cup the ash of our bodies.

I was born despite the myth that I would die.
They should have cut his cock to size, shaved it like metal.

Occasionally we eat pork. My mother eats my father
and my father eats my brother and my sister eats
the brown mess underneath the meat.

Pigs breathe in the same air as people.
Crash into their flesh like roads into a mountain.

When I came out, they held me over holy water.
My father rolled up his sleeves in heat. My mother
opened her hands like a trap:

Be brave with me.

Laurentian Figures

I sit with strangers
in open rooms.

Stale air,
constant talk.

I decide the day I die.

.

Brushes of soft fur
in the library of dead timber.

Blankets once draped
over bone.

.

Reading verses on leather couches.
Pages will go
in one ear and out the other.

I hope, finally, this once.

.

I see a fox in the garden bed.
Neither of us know what we'll do.

I think about thinking about the burn of bushes
and about thinking about thinking about
the burning of it all.

A letter forgotten in the mail.

.

My life has become a photograph
saddled by dead light in the quad
under electric wires.

.

I double underline my eyes with red marker
found on my roommate's desk.

Texture of plates and seafoam.

.

He leaves to put on a sweater
and when he returns

his eyes go red with blood
as he dances on my corpse.

.

Boredom sits
alone
in a
chair
with the
sun pulled
down
to the
floor.

.

Time tends to non-being as a thought.
The impression of what's slipping away
and what to long for.

.

I wait for the bus
with the other lonely people
because they're my brothers and sisters

but don't think I won't leave them.

.

A parking lot gate closed when the sign says open.
A parking lot gate open when the sign says closed.

.

I eat lunch at the strip mall
when I see a man hug his daughter.

I haven't seen you in so long, she said.

He embraces her
for what seems like forever.

It's all so boring.

.

Highlighting lines in books
to never read again.

The future doesn't exist if
I am the future.

Just wait.

.

In the mail
a photograph of a raven
perched on a telephone.

This is the best *fuck you*
I've ever seen.

.

Sitting outside when
a ladybug lands on my arm.

Maybe this is a sign
to begin my life
in the spring.

I find out
the room above me
is infested with them.

.

Happiness is something you choose
like a sweater or a pair of shoes.

If you can't choose happiness
remember that you'll live forever.

.

Today I pack everything.
Ready to leave this place.

The walls are blank.
The shelves are empty.

Finally this room is a mirror.

When I Get Lonely

When I get lonely, I spit in people's faces.
They ask for it and breathe a sigh of relief.

I do it all day and carelessly.
My tongue like a knife, open in branded fur, my torso

like a dusty moth under the fake-fuck moonlight.
When people get lonely, they tell me how powerful they are

and paralyzed –
Sometimes they speak in tongues and convulse

like winded trees. The Good Holy Father speaks in signs,
like born-again saints. The Good Holy Father fingers wounds

from books and glues pages shut. When I get happy,
I pull hair and sweep glitter from my mattress. I mould glitter

into a ball and lick my palms clean, discard shards
in the toilet. When I get boring, I shove cigarettes

in my urethra and carve holes from digits.
I have been black-eyed and staggered, but honestly,

it's too late now.
All the empty spaces

fill with balloons of blood. To be born, I had to fall
from great heights, be fucked by a highway of a million hands.

The Good Holy Mother of the Room sacrifices herself to the world,
tells me she has never been real.

Dog Dick

I kneel on the lips of ancient kings.

Royal blue jackets wet in the death of horseshoe crabs.

Oversized luxurious beds for dogs to die in.

Like puzzles carefully considered on Sundays, needles on
thread, where the sun shines down on all animals.

We pick tomatoes thrown by the onlookers at our hanging.

Public display of ripe and ready ghosts.

The dog has a dick.

Ride the red rocket into dusk.

Mary.

The Lord, our Father.

When I walk to the park on dog days.

Coffee harder than bullets, highways out and back
into town, going anywhere.

Hidden coleus.

Cum trees.

Cut off pieces of the black ribbon.

For good behaviour, best effort,
milking the prized animal, the drained specimen.

Skyscrapers bloom above legends in valleys of concrete,
among bodies of the dead.

The abattoir is full.

Freshly shaved beards on enamel tile.

Leather leashes hung on barn nails.

I will live forever among their scent.

Beneath the golden hems of kings.

Poetry Ruins My Life

I was a relay sprinter but would
rather describe running.
Fingers bled on birthdays.
Twelve years ago, on the shores of a lake.
I could gut a fish but not devour it.
Shot a bullet through a moose with a rifle.
Still bolted up in a box.
Red prints on book corners.
Slow motion fall of the calf.
Ran out of the woods alone with a loose heart.
I never shot a damn moose.
I apologize.

Vow

Silence feels good throughout the seasons.
Dried flowers, snow and tree trunks
shoved into my neck at morning.
I was born with a fist in my abdomen
and I was silent when they laid me out.
All their hands smashed onto my torso
by nightfall and I remember
running into the tamaracks, all of them
burned down, and I asked the firefighters,
How do I become a part of this? My name is
Joshua Chris, given to me by perverted
children in the backyard. I learned to hold birds
by the neck, and I knew how to shovel skin,
suck dirty water from old green hoses.
We kept dogs in the basement and we
shut the bedroom door to do drugs and throw
flints at the floor. We put the sun's mouth
on our genitals, where freckles came from,
everything we did like patterns, and I am
not surprised anymore. Now I wear the proof.
Some days at dusk I put a stereo on the stoop
and dance for my friends made of wood,
spit at their feet, and the men come to sing
like drunk kings in their shamelessness.
I don't have all the answers but
I can still ease to bloom in all that I suck
from open things. Eyes wired in fishing line
and golden rings. Nothing I mourn will be sacred.

Acknowledgements

Thank you to my friends who have supported me all these years: Jessica Bebenek, Elizabeth Burns, MLA Chernoff, Jordan Eady, JM Francheteau, Jay Ryan G., Meghan Harrison, Alex Hood, Jo Ianni, Zak Jones, Chris Johnson, Sophie McCreesh, Jesse Menard, Khashayar "Kess" Mohammadi and Fawn Parker. Thank you to my editor, Liz Howard, for her thoughtfulness and care for this book, and everyone at Wolsak and Wynn. Mia, I love you.

Thank you to the journals where the following poems, or versions of them, have previously appeared:

Acta Victoriana: "Monuments"
The Ampersand Review: "Black Fly"
Bad Nudes: "Birds Fly into the Mouth of the Sun"; "Animals"
Carousel: "Nil by Mouth"
carte blanche: "Dissemination"
Deathcap: "Letters to Lost Children"
Echolocation: "Stet"
Event: "Leaf Blower"
The Ex-Puritan: "What I May Have Been if I had Been There"
Half a Grapefruit: "All the Places Look Like Forest Fires"
Ice Floe Press: "Burial"
Poetry Is Dead: "How to Tear a Partridge Apart"
PRISM international: "I Am Well"
Soliloquies Anthology: "Heritage Site"

I acknowledge the support of the Ontario Arts Council.

Joshua Chris Bouchard is the author of *Let This Be the End of Me* (Bad Books Press) shortlisted for the 2019 bpNichol Chapbook Award. He wrote or cowrote five chapbooks, and his poetry appears in *Event, CV2, Carousel, Poetry Is Dead, PRISM international, Arc, The Ex-Puritan* and more.